BELOVED

emma farry

Te whenua he whaea

e kore e mate

The land is the mother

that never dies

—

Mãori Proverb

For Pamela Farry

12 July 1940 – 18 March 2013

When my beloved mother Pamela died in 2013 I took my sorrow to a rock at the end of Karitane beach in Otago, Aotearoa, New Zealand.

The large rock pictured on page 17 of this book was a patient teacher when I was angry, sad, confused and mourning.

Daily I dragged my aching, broken-hearted self through the necessities of the day, counting the hours until I could climb up onto my rock. I was soothed by a sense of her deep silence and nurtured by her surprising wisdom.

I spent many hours sitting up there, breathing deeply, meditating, crying, coming to terms with the depth of my loss. For two years I watched the tides come in and out, and the seasons change. In summer I basked in the sun and in winter I endured the howling winds, and when hailstones rained down on me I smiled at my own desperation.

Through the grace of those hours and the deep acceptance I felt in that sacred space, I was able to forge a new relationship with myself. I was also relieved to find Pamela inside my heart, where she had been waiting all along.

These blessings and a new love of photography emerged from my time on the rock. I hope they give you the comfort and strength they have given me.

Emma Farry

The wound is

the place where the

light enters you.

—

Jalāl ad-Dīn Muhammad Rūmī

1207 - 1273

Karitane Estuary, Otago

◆

Beloved,

Thank you for the dependable rhythm of the tides. Thank you for the way they come in with steady confidence and certainty and for the way they draw back into the vastness with a swiftness that never seems hurried.

Thank you most especially for the point of stillness when the tide has reached her fullness or the bottom of her emptiness.

Thank you for the deep silent pause of this moment.

Help us to find this same still place within the comings and goings of our own emotional tides and to rest there when the weather of our human life is rough and troubled.

Muriwai Beach, Auckland

◆

Dear friend,

Thank you for our overwhelming expectations and the feelings of panic they create in us.

Be with us as we examine our responsibilities and our feelings about them, and decide which burdens we may drop and which we must strengthen ourselves to bear.

Muriwai Beach, Auckland

◆

Beloved,

Thank you for each and every tree. Thank you for their quiet and comforting strength and for the patience they display by their very being.

When the day is long and filled with pain, help us to take time to sit against a trunk and listen to the tree's soothing, loving counsel.

May we learn in the silent certainty and faith of the tree that stillness, gentle breathing and a deep connection to Mother Earth can solve many of our problems.

Muriwai Campground, Auckland

◆

Dearest friend,

Thank you for our weaknesses, those parts of us that struggle just to get through the day. Help us to spend time exploring those parts of ourselves that we believe are unworthy of love.

Hold our hands, compassionate one, as we travel to our darkest places and make friends with the lonely strangers we have ignored for so long.

Shine your light on us as we make room inside ourselves for those stories we have formerly shunned. Help us to embrace our darkness, just as we struggle to embrace our light. Let us understand that in your eyes each part of us is equally lovable and deserving of compassion.

Karitane Beach, Otago

◆

Beloved,

Thank you for the people who exasperate us, who make us angry, who violate our boundaries, who have no self-awareness.

Thank you for the mirror they hold up for us and the feelings of anger that rise up within us in their presence. Help us to acknowledge and to forgive.

Bless them and bless us when we sense the insight they provide us with.

Help us to find a balance between honouring our feelings, and surrendering to your perfect and non-judgmental love.

Muriwai Beach, Auckland

◆

Beloved,

Thank you for our roots that grow down deep into your fertile earth. Help us to never forget the gift of life that flows from you and nourishes us in the often unknown depths of our being.

Sit with us, wise one, as we travel down into those depths and rest with you in the peaceful foundations of our own human lives. Guide our roots to your underground streams that give us the sustenance we need to grow strong.

Gentle one, root us to your earth. Show each one of us how to connect with your presence beneath our feet and to be anchored here while we grow slowly and steadily towards the light.

Muriwai Sand Dunes, Auckland

My friend,

Thank you for the wind. For the way it caresses our skin on a sunny day and for the way it whips around us in winter when the sun has gone.

Thank you for the way the wind keeps the cloudy sky ever-changing and for the way it coaxes the leaves gently from the trees in their final, swirling dance.

Thank you for the way the wind blows away our old, unwanted habits and for the movement that draws us always back into the dance of our lives.

Muriwai Beach, Auckland

◆

Beloved,

Thank you that we can hear the sounds of nature as they gently soften our minds and nurture our souls. Thank you for the love we hear in the voices of our families and friends.

Thank you too for the gift of silence. Thank you for the space it creates inside us and for the soothing voices it allows us to hear from the inside.

Thank you for the sounds of this world and the silence of this world.

Be with us as we use our ears to balance them.

Maukatia Bay, Auckland

◆

Beloved,

Thank you for the way our tears
empty us of our pain and bring us
back to the present moment.

Be with us as we weep for those
we have lost, and as we weep for
ourselves as we go on living
without them.

Thank you that we can connect with
ourselves enough to enable us to
express our pain through our tears.

We ask you to cradle us, wise one,
as we navigate our grief and our
loss and our sorrows.

Help us to shed our tears with
abandon and with passion, and to
know that after the rainstorm the
earth sparkles.

Muriwai Beach, Auckland

My beloved,

Thank you for the colourful, crunchy leaves of autumn.

Thank you for the thrill of walking through them, and for the way they make their own deaths so very beautiful.

◆

Beloved,

Thank you for our complaints.

Thank you for their honesty and for
their ability to keep us humble.

Thank you that they point to our truth
and to the things in our lives we must
either accept or change.

May we honour our complaints and be
unashamed of our need to voice them.

May we find within them the way
back to the equilibrium that at times
eludes us.

Arorangi Beach, Cook Islands

◆

Beloved,

Thank you for our frailties, for those places within us that seem to resist your grace so effectively.

Give us the strength to enliven those deadened places. Be with us as we examine our mistaken belief that we will never be good enough, that we are flawed beyond redemption.

Sit with us as we befriend those difficult parts of ourselves that keep moving just beyond our reach. Give us the courage to listen to our own stories of shame.

Be with us as we sit with them quietly, as we acknowledge their presence, as we love them.

Give us the strength to embrace the whole of ourselves, shame and all.

Woodhill Forrest, Auckland

Dearest friend,

Help us to balance our love for others
with our love for ourselves.

Help us to understand that it is not
selfish to look after ourselves, merely
something that must be done if we
wish to live balanced and truly
loving lives.

Be with us as we bring our needs
and our dreams into the picture of
our lives, and honour our own inner
guidance.

Shelly Beach, Karitane, Otago

Beloved,

Thank you for our passions, for those things that thrill us and quench our deep thirst for life.

May we find your friendly presence within all those things that we truly love, and feel your hand guiding our own as we create and compose and collaborate.

◆

Beloved,

When we are weary with life and its demands, help us to take the time we need to rest. Remind us of our great worth and comfort us when this world takes its toll on our sensitive souls.

Lie with us as we relax and nap and sleep, and help us not to forget to treat ourselves kindly, with deep respect and great reverence.

◆

My friend,

Thank you for our inner doubts.

Thank you that one day we can think we are certain about something and then the next day that we are not so sure at all.

Help us not to cling too tightly to our opinions and beliefs and to know that when we take ourselves too seriously, you will always find a way to nudge us gently from our pedestals.

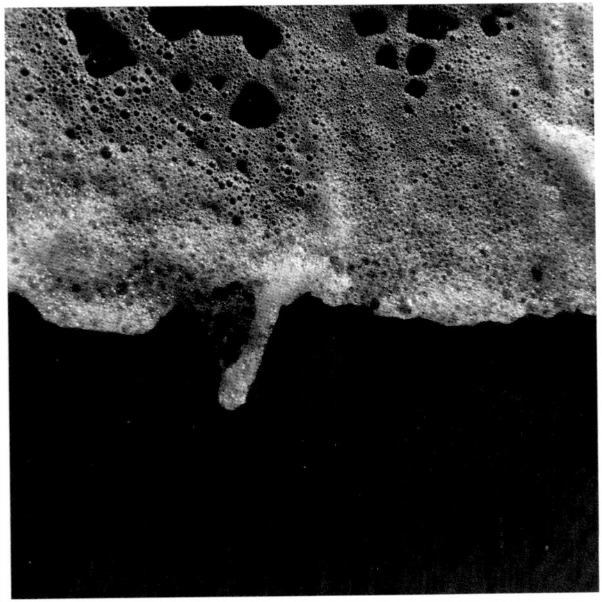

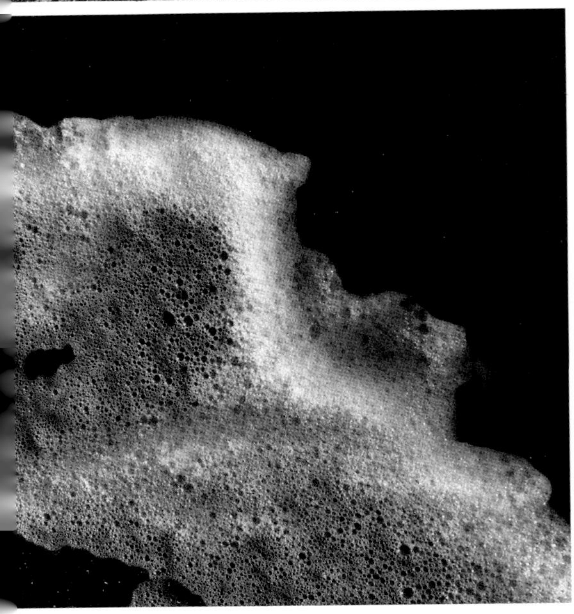

Beloved,

There never seems to be enough time
to achieve all we desire.

Help us to give ourselves a break
from life's demands.

Help us to understand that we need
not achieve and strive every day, but
that we can learn to live slowly, with
deep gratitude, and to allow our lives
to unfold as they will.

Be with us as we birth our new selves,
as we act as a patient midwife to a life
of wholehearted, peaceful presence.

Arorangi Beach, Cook Islands

◆

Dearest friend,

Thank you for our pain. Thank you for the way it grounds us in our bodies and forces us to turn within. Thank you for the way it humbles us, how it points towards a life of true compassion.

Thank you that our own pain helps us to finally understand the pain of others, and relegates our righteousness to dust.

Be with us as we journey to the centre of our pain and explore the wisdom that lies there waiting patiently for our attention.

Help us to listen respectfully to the stories stored within our pain, and to acknowledge them for the sacred messengers that they are.

Domain Crescent, Muriwai Beach, Auckland

Beloved,

Thank you for those loved ones who have finished with their human bodies. Be with us as we mourn them, embrace us as we finally let them go. When our hearts are aching and breaking, help us to believe that they are breaking open as well as apart and that there will be brighter days to come.

When we yearn for our loved one, when we curl up with a piece of their clothing and inhale their scent, let us know that we will see them again. Remind us that their body, which we love so much, is only a small part of who they have now become.

◆

Arorangi Beach, Cook Islands

Beloved:

Be love

Be loved.

My mother Pamela was the first person to call me a writer. When I was nine she gathered my poems together and wrote them into a hard-covered red journal in her spidery yet sophisticated cursive. This act of faith is the bedrock of my continued willingness to return to the page.

Now Pamela is gone I have my own little hard-cover book to offer, and I know that she is playing a large role in getting it into your hands.

emmafarry.com

ISBN 978-0-473-36272-0

First published 2016

Published by Be Loved Press Ltd

86 Waitea Rd, Muriwai Beach, Auckland 0881, New Zealand

For further copies or comments please email me@emmafarry.com

Designed by Wade Wu

Edited by Geoff Walker

Printed in China through Asia Pacific Offset